Ladies Forget What You've Heard, The Uncut Truth About What Men Really Think!

A Woman's guide to better understanding, What goes on in the minds of Men.

By: Yamo

First published by Dog Ear Publishing
4010 W. 86th Street, Ste H
Indianapolis, IN 46268
www.dogearpublishing.net

ISBN: 1-59858-179-1

This book is printed on acid-free paper.

Printed in the United States of America

Ladies, Forget What You've Heard, The Uncut Truth About What Men Really Think!

Dedication:

This book is dedicated to my Beautiful wife and bestfriend Darlisa. Your love, support, and inspiration are the reason I'm here. You believed in me when I didn't believe in myself, I love you!

Next are my three beautiful daughters: Marquita, Brandy, and Tiahna, the three of you are the light of my life, and will forever be Daddy's Little Girls.

My son Isaiah (Zay), I strive to give you someone to look up to, and always be able to turn to.

My siblings; DeAngelo (Lo), Ayesha, Ashanti, and Mikkel, I just want to make you proud, we've been through a lot and better days are finally here.

My mothers' (The one who birthed me & the one's who helped raise me): Joy, Khalila, Toni, Lonnie, Shirley, Dorothy, Margaret, and Wanda, they say it takes a village to raise a child and you ladies did a hell of a job! After all the gray hairs I've given all of you over the years I pray I've finally given you something to smile about.

To all my <u>true</u> friends who never turned their backs on me, rode the storms out with me, and believed in me, thank you and I love you!

In loving memory of those who God called home before I finally got it right in life; Pops, Nana, Ramadan, Grandpa Downing, and Larry Stringer, I love & miss you all so very much.

Yamo

—*Intro*—

Ladies, the time has finally come. The time to bring you out of the darkness, and shine some light on what goes on in the minds of men. Everything that you thought you knew, you can toss it out the window. You thought you knew Lady you have No clue. See, if you Absolutely understood how the male mind ticked, your first relationship would ultimately have been your last. The two of you would be living happily ever after to this very day and you wouldn't be reading this book. Considering the fact that you're still reading only further confirms the fact that you know if you desire to have a successful relationship with a man you need to fully understand him. As you continue to comb these pages, don't be surprised to find yourself saying things like; "No wonder", "I understand now", "That's why", "I didn't know", and "Ain't that a Bitch", among other things.

That, which I'm giving you within these pages, won't be found in any medical journals. These aren't the opinions of any MD's, or PHD, or any other per-

son with a title who thinks that they know. If you ask any man and they are completely honest, you'll see that this is real not speculation. What I'm bringing to you is the uncut truth of what goes on in the minds of men from real men. In this book I will break "Male Codes" in a sincere effort to give women the tools they need in order to not only get it, but keep it right!

Your question: "Why would any Man violate these masculine codes, and pull the veil off of what goes on in the minds of men?" In three words... Because I can! By the end of this book you will encounter many truths that for some reason men never tell, and many lies that men often tell. Most of all you'll have a clear and concise understanding as to why; Men do or don't, reveal or hide, say or plead the fifth. You will have the uncut truth about what men really think.

So walk with me as I take you on a journey into the minds of men. Be warned however, that the UNCUT truth is often shocking, hard hitting, and a tough pill to swallow in many instances. Brace yourself and don't stop turning these pages until you reach the end. By the last page you may be; happy, perhaps sad, one might be embarrassed, another moist, but all will be enlightened!

Now let's go...

Chapter 1: Attraction

No matter what you've been told or led to believe prior today, I'm here to inform you that the first attraction is 9 1/2 times out of 10 physical.

It wasn't your brains, but your booty. Forget your social, or economic class, your degrees or nice personality, what attracted me to you in the door was absolutely physical. Every other quality that you possess that you felt make you a good catch is a distant second on the list. Regardless of the analogy, know that every man has his preferred taste, i.e. what he looks for in a woman. At the top of that list will be his physical desire. We seek our "Eye Candy" first; all else falls in line afterwards.

That being said, a fact that can't be stressed enough: The same cares that it took to get you there, it definitely takes to keep you there. The things that you did in an effort to make yourself appealing during the courting or dating phase should definitely be maintained after the catch has been made. Please stop fooling yourself into thinking that just because we're together now that you don't have to be my "Eye Candy". If you feel that now you can just let yourself go you've just fucked up! That which attracted me to you is what keeps me wanting you. Remember that it was the physical that was the initial attraction! The little things you did in the beginning in an effort to keep me coming back for more, it takes "At Least" that much effort to keep me focused on only you. When you fall off thus goes our focus! We don't wander because we have to, or because we want to, but solely because your actions or lack there of allow us to!

- *If you were getting your hair and nails done every other week, don't stop.*

- *If you were dedicating four days a week to working out, don't let the health club membership or the workout tapes collect dust.*

- *If Vicki Secretes was your sleep wear of choice to heat me up, don't freeze me out with those itchy ass flannel pajamas or those ugly torn up jogging pants.*

- *If you started out putting your foot in those pots in the kitchen, don't start slacking with the microwave or fast food gourmet meals.*

- *If you were fucking my brains out at the drop of a dime in the beginning, lose the headaches, because they're giving me one.*

These are just a few examples, but I'm more than certain you can fully grasp the message that I'm conveying. Keep your game tight and we won't have to go out to play.

Ladies hold tight to this truth; although our first attraction to you was a physical one, my brother Shaughnessy said it best with this one quote. "A pretty face only lasts two weeks, now what else you got?" If a pretty face is all that you have to bring to the table, then don't bother sitting down because you won't be here long. No matter how shallow you've been led to believe the male psyche is, truth be told we do seek more than just a show piece.

A few of our must have characteristics:

- <u>*Secure*</u>*: If you've earned the position of the one and only, know that you're there for a reason. The reason being because we want you there! If we wanted another woman there she would be and not you. A touch of jealously is flattering. It lets us know that you really do care about what you've got, and don't want another woman* *sniffing around your back door. Note, anything done in excess is going to do more harm than good. Too much jealousy especially unwarranted will turn us off faster than the Power Company two weeks after an unpaid final notice.*

- *Honest: No one likes a liar. Secretes will always be construed as a lie. If I can't trust you, and your word is no good, you'll never mean anything to me.*

- *Mature: Age has absolutely nothing to do with being mature. Men define a mature woman as; one who embarks on a situation with not only an open mind but also a desire to work towards a solution amicable to all parties involved. If you are the type that feels your opinion or resolution is the only correct one, the most compatible person for you to be in a relationship with is yourself.*

- *Passionate: Always do what it takes to be the object of my desire, and make sure that I'm the object of yours. Take steps daily to reinforce in my mind that I am the one you want. Be a perfect lady in the streets and an absolute freak when we close the bedroom door.*

- *<u>Balanced</u>: Every man wants a woman who can keep a good home. We also want you to be out going so that we can enjoy one another away from home as well. We don't want a street runner, nor do we want a couch potato but a nice balance between the two.*

- *<u>Sense of Humor</u>: Who wants an uptight partner? Be able to relax, laugh, and enjoy life.*

- *<u>Goal Oriented</u>: If you have no goals you're informing us that you have no future, and we can stumble through life just fine by ourselves. Believe it or not we are well aware of the fact that behind every great man stands an even greater woman. O if you have no goals or have fallen short of achieving yours, how in the world could you attempt to help me with mine? If you have no goals we have no future.*

- *<u>Loving</u>: Love me for my shortcomings as well as my successes. Love me unconditionally in good and bad times. Make me know that your love is given not bought and paid for. Don't just tell me that you love me, show me and* *show me often!*

- <u>*Dependable*</u>*: Convince me that you've got my back 110%. Etch in stone that you will hold me down against any odds and under any pressure and not falter. Assure me that I can always count on you and you'll always be the first person I turn to, whatever the situation.*

- <u>*Communication*</u>*: Talk to me about anything. If you can't lay all your cards on the table for me then you must have some cuffed and no one likes a shady card player. Communication is one of the cornerstones of any relationship. If we can't defuse a situation through communication it will evolve into something much worse. Contrary to what you've been told, we hate to fight with our woman.*

- <u>*Sexy not sleazy*</u>*: Every man desires a woman with class. How much class you need depends on his school of thought. You are a reflection of us as we are of you. We want a woman who will represent us well in public. Conduct yourself like a lady. Dress sexy not sleazy, damn leave something to the imagination. A* *dress with a split up the side gives us an occasional peek at your thigh is sexy, a skirt that is so short that you're tugging at the hem all night and if you bend over we'll see what you ate for breakfast is sleazy. A blouse that compliments your curves and caresses your breast is sexy. Your little sister's shirt that cuts off the circulation from the waist up just to bring attention to your breast is sleazy. Try just enough make up to high light and compliment your true beauty as opposed to so much that you've painted over your true beauty and look like an absolute clown.*

Ladies you never get a second chance to make a first impression and your physical impression is the first one that you give. One of my mothers (Toni) used to tell us "If you bring your friends home, I can tell you who you are." This can be applied to women with regards to dress. The way you dress will determine the type of men you attract. Any man can approach a sleazy dressed woman, but no man will approach a woman that he feels is out of his league. If properly maintained, that which attracted me to you will keep me with you. If your level of maintenance falls off, so will your hold on our attention. The care that it took to get you there, at minimum it will take to keep you there. My advise to you Ladies; keep your shit tight and don't ever get complacent. There is always a woman waiting in the wings to pickup the slack in the areas that you lack!

Chapter 2: Mental and Emotional

Men do not equate love with sex! Women most often use sex to get love and men use love to get sex. If you look up either word in the dictionary, neither is the definition of the other. Ladies no matter how cold you think you are, pussy alone is never enough to make a man fall in love. Lose the notion that you can fuck a man into submission, "<u>*Not going to happen*</u>*"! All you will accomplish with this mentality is; becoming some convenient sex, and two becoming emotionally hooked in the process. If you work hard on getting the head on my shoulders to fall in love with you the one in my pants will be more than happy to follow. With a mental and emotional connection the sex will evolve into lovemaking.*

Ladies, Men have been accused of many things, but we are Not, have Not been, and Never ever will we be mind readers! Stop assuming that we know what's on your mind! Just tell us what you're thinking or how you feel, it eliminates any room for misunderstanding. Simple communication is the ultimate mechanism need to avoid conflict. Rule of thumb: Communicate don't let it marinade! Open your damn mouth and talk to us. Let me emphasize "Talk To Us", "Not At Us"! No matter how we may act at times, we are not kids and we don't work for you, so we are to be talked to not at. When we're talked at our defense mechanisms automatically kick in and we have a natural inclination to resist whatever. When you talk at us you give off the aura that your position within the relationship is bigger than ours and you're attempting to belittle us. Ladies we hate to feel that someone is attempting to put their foot on us, especially our mate. So it's as simple as thinking before you speak and talking to us instead of at us.

<u>*Do Not*</u> *under any circumstances attempt to talk to us about anything of importance under the following conditions; after multiple drinks, while we're watching a sporting event, in front of others, and especially during sex (regular or oral) we're subject to tell you anything! Schedule a time to dialogue where it's just the two of us, in a relaxed atmosphere, and allow nothing to distract you until the conversation is done. Turn of the television, the phones (cell and house), ask the kids not to disturb and talk to your man, and you'll find that we'll be honest and open.*

If there are two facts that I can't stress enough in this book; <u>Men absolutely hate to be nagged, and</u>

<u>positively hate to argue with our mate!</u> We get enough brow bashing from the world on a daily basis; the last thing we want to encounter when we come home is a nagging and argumentative woman. Mentally and emotionally, arguing and nagging stresses us and drains us of so much energy. If this is something that we're subjected to more often than not we'll get to the point that we'd rather be anywhere but there. The more you argue and nag the more you remind us that our ex wasn't so bad after all! A few tell tale signs that you're arguing with or nagging your man too much:

- *When he arrives home he begins drinking and doesn't stop until he or you fall asleep.*

- *He begins saying things to you that he's never said before like, "Shut the fuck up", Get out", "I'm out of here", "Fuck you", just to name a few. But you get the point!*

- *He never comes straight home anymore, and when he arrives he's intoxicated.*

- *When you call him at work or on his cell phone you get his voice mail more often than you get him.*

- *The television has become much more*

exciting than you have.

- *Sex become straight and to the point.*

You are supposed to be our best friend, lover, and number one supporter. We have no desire to constantly argue with you or be nagged by you. We consider home as our safe haven, our place of peace, tranquility, and refuge. If we can't find peace at home, we'll have no desire to be there. Nagging and arguing chips away at the foundation of a relationship until it eventually crumbles. When we get to the point that we tell you that, "We are tired, and have had enough" you are half way out the door. My advise: If you are unable to talk situations out without arguing, if you constantly feel the need to nag, you have too much aggression built up and you need to find a punching bag other than your man or you can bet you or him is out of there.

Learn our struggles; inquire about our troubles sometimes instead of always bombarding us with yours. We often feel the weight of the world on our shoulders and need some relief. Our relief doesn't come from you trying to solve our problems. All you need to do to help ease our pain is listen without interruption or suggestion. Just let us lay our head in your lap and vent, as we vent gently rub our head. Then when we're done just tell us, that you are with us and it's going to be all right. When necessary build us back up by stroking our ego. Most often these little

*things are all the relief we need, and energizes us
enough that we're ready to face the world again. Best
of all however, it reveals to us that you care about our
pain and are there for us.*

Chapter 3: Acceptance

Men correlate acceptance with that which will or won't be allowed within the relationship, basically the dos and don'ts. Our biggest "Don't" with regards to women's actions is; don't accept anything on day one that you aren't willing to accept on day one hundred and one, day one thousand and one and so on. The first question we'll ask is, "We're you being phony then or are you being phony now"? Did you accept certain things in an effort to get me, and now that you have me those things aren't acceptable anymore? The flip-flop behavior doesn't sit well with us and we'd like the real you to please stand up. Once the real you stands up we can decide if we want to stay with you or do we like the old you so much that the new you is unacceptable and we no longer want to be with this new you. Be honest and up front about what you will and won't accept and stand firm on it because believe me we will.

If we can pull it, we absolutely will. What this means is that if we commit an action and you allow it, then we've set it in our minds that it's allowed, and when ever we're ready then we'll do it again. If we do something that you don't like, let it be known then and there that it's unacceptable to you and hold your ground. Otherwise be prepared for us to pull it again, give us an inch and we won't hesitate to run a marathon.

Ladies, when you've come to a point in the relationship that some sort of changes needs to be made, first step is to suggest change, second the two of you together plot a course towards the desired goal. Don't demand change, because like ultimatums, demands trigger our defense mechanisms. Your demand may even have validity, but just because you made it a demand or an ultimatum we'll resist it just because. We don't do Ultimatums or demands period! Change has to be worked towards equally by both parties, not demanded by one and implemented by the other. Remember that this is a relationship not a dictatorship!

Next to lying and cheating the next big no no that no man will stomach is to be compared negatively to another man. Don't ever highlight my shortcomings by comparing them to the lack there of in another man, especially your ex or someone else's man. If you enjoy their qualities that much, then by chance that's the one that you need to be with!

From day one, a man will voice that, which he will or won't allow into a relationship, so should you.

Or are you under the guise that if it's not mentioned it's ok? You can best believe that that is our outlook. Starting off lax then attempting to stern up down the line will only lead to conflict. If you don't like it don't accept it; if you accept it once then enjoy it forever. When you feel that you are tired of accepting it then enjoy the disdain and resentment that comes with your sudden change in position.

Chapter 4: Physical

If you're selling ass set a price and get on with it! As harsh as it may sound, you'll understand the point if you just keep reading. It has long been the practice of many men who can't talk up on sex to attempt to pay for it. A certain R&B singer legitimized the behavior with a song talking about what he'll pay for as soon as he got home from work. Over time, men who fell into this category were given titles such as; "Sugar Daddy, Cake, Pay Master, and Trick, to name a few". Ladies don't get it twisted, we are fully aware of the arrangement. Don't think that you're doing anything slick to a can of oil! When a man kicks out money to you for; rent, car note, vacation, a trip to the mall, a night on the town, car repair, hairdo, nails done, the baby's day care, it's a down payment on a shot of ass! Understand that we are absolutely conscious of two things; One is that we're paying for ass, and two is that you're selling ass as soon as you fix your mouth to ask me for money for any of the above and we aren't in a heart felt committed relationship.

The only thing we ask is that if financial gain is the only reason that you're in my face pleasing be woman enough to do the following:

- *Be open and up front about it in the door.*

- *Negotiate an amicable price.*

- *Set a date and time for us to fuck.*

- *Once we fuck I hand you your payment and we go our separate ways.*

Remember that we're all adults. We hate when you drag out what could ultimately be a one-day affair, into months of cat and mouse. You didn't honestly think that your game was that tight and we didn't know what you were up to? So accept the fact that if you fall into this category that you are indeed selling ass. So if you are, be woman enough to admit it up front and let's get it over with.

Ladies, this next subject is something near and dear to men and you need to be well aware of. Men don't do well on rations! Sex can not be rationed out to us, nor can it be used as a bargaining tool. Men desires sex, and desire it often. If you attempt to hold it back, ration it out, or barter with it we'll go seek it out else where, but be sure we won't do without! Fuck us well and often and you won't have to worry about us roaming.

Try this, instead of fussing when we are about to go out with the fellas, fuck us good before we go and be ready to break us off again when we return. Rest assured, you would be the only thing that we're thinking about while we are out. Not to mention you'll find that we'll probably be home sooner than expected. Stop rationing out the sex, or trying to use it as carrot on a stick. We are very aware that there are many more carrots in the garden with no strings attached to them. Rations will make us rotate!

Release your inhibitions! Keep it spicy! There is nothing worse than boring sex. A man would rather endure a root canal then boring sex. If you don't trust your man enough to completely open up sexually, then by chance you might be with the wrong man! There is an erotic side to every woman, but many keep it suppressed for one of two reasons. One reason is for fear of it being exploited by her man or two for fear that once released she can't control it. All I can say is, release it ladies and keep the relationship spicy. A spicy relationship will keep a man coming back for more.

Take the wheel and drive often. When we have a take charge (we're not talking about some domina-trix) woman in the bedroom, it ignites a fire inside us. A little aggression on your behalf informs us that we are desired physically. Men have no problem getting in the passengers seat and turning the wheel over to you and admiring your stick shift skills.

If you truly want a man to be satisfying to you sexually, then forget the trail, error, and a potentially disappointing experience and just tell us how you like it. You will find that we are quick studies, and have ample memory to store the instructions for future use. By directing us to your hot spots, ideal tempo, stroke preference, and favorite position will make for a much more memorable experience, guaranteed! Nothing would please us more than to see our woman smiling, curled up in the fetal position after multiple breath-taking orgasms, whispering, "Don't touch me, just let me lay here"! So don't let us stumble around in the dark, guide us to your light and we'll get there often.

In a committed relationship the word <u>No</u> is off limits in the bedroom! Always be willing, because if you won't, we'll seek out someone who will. You can believe that there are women out there that will do everything I want you to do and some things I never thought of. Men are well aware of the boundaries in the relationship, and will make very few special requests. The ones that we do make should be promptly and wholeheartedly adhered to, in the name of pleasing your man. Ladies if you deny us, attempt to ration us, carrot on a stick us, you'll notice we'll have a headache more often than you ever had. Not to mention we will be finding pleasure in another, liter-ally. My advice: Keep us creatively and consistently well fucked and you'll have few problems out of us.

Chapter 5: Security

Relationships:

Be secure, not comfortable. Ladies know that you've earned the position as the lady in his life, but be well aware that keeping the spot is a continuos working process. Remember chapter one, the care that it took to get you here, it takes at least that much to keep you there. Be forever mindful that when you have something good, there are always others lurking in the wings, patiently waiting for you to slack so that they can ease in and pick up in the areas that you lack. Complacency on your behalf will always open the door for another to whisper in our ear and tell us something that we want or need to hear. If a farmer wants to reap a harvest, he must not only plant the seeds but he must also be ever vigilant tending to his crops. In a nut shell, be secure in your relationship, know that he's your man and will continue to be *because you do what is need to ensure no other seeds get planted on your land.*

Financial:

Build financial security together, or you'll build a wedge. If we are under the notion that the money that you earn is yours and the money I earn is ours, the usury alarm is activated. If you know how much I bring home and I'm clueless as to your earnings it puts some space in between us. If we can't set financial goals for the relationship, open a joint account (not withstanding our individual accounts), and work together towards achieving the goals, the wedge has been built. See, if you are unwilling to build together financially, the impression that you give is that this is not where you plan to be in the future.

Physically:

Hold me down when times are rough, or I'm up once they get good. Stop being fair weather women. As long as things are good you love my dirty drawers, but at the fist signs of rough seas you grab a life raft and jump ship then try to come back when the storm subsides. We pay close

Attention to how you hold up under pressure. If we see that you stray or falter, the relationship is over you just don't know it yet. We simply bide our time until the situation changes for the better then we notify you that we've come to the end of the road. We plotted our exit the very moment that you faltered. Truly have our back (not so far back that we have to call on you by phone) and hold us down through any situation and we'll definitely do the same if not more for you. Enduring tough times together strengthens a relationship if both parties stand strong. In every relationship some rain will fall, so either weather the storm with your man. If you can't stand the rain, then wash out to sea so that I can cast my line and make a catch worth keeping, because you proved to be a throw back

Chapter 6: Spiritual

Religion is something that can't be force fed, and there should be no compulsion in religion. We all may not jump up and clap in church, or attend jummah prayer every Friday, but please don't question the level of our spirituality.

Two simple rules when dealing with spirituality and a man:

- *Keep God first. This is the absolute best foundation to build upon. God comes first and your mate is second <u>only</u> to God. Just be ever mindful of God when dealing with your man and you'll always treat him right.*

- *Respect one another's beliefs. Don't allow a difference in religious beliefs divide you. Seek out the similarities and build upon them instead of allowing the differences drive a wedge.*

God created man and woman to be together.
So work on reasons and ways to be together instead of
inventing reasons to be apart.

Chapter 7: Outsiders

Allowing outsiders into a relationship will destroy it faster than any destructive force known to man. If you let a snake into your home, some one will ultimately get bit. Once the poison from the bite has been released, the antidote if found in time is painful and slow working. Often times the poison spewed by Outsiders is fatal to a relationship.

- *Keep Other's Philosophies out of the Equation: All decisions made in the relationship are to be made between you and him. Therefor the only opinions that ever matter are yours and mine. Misery loves company; so don't let other's issues under mind what you've built.*

- *You are in this relationship with him, only you. Only the woman who's fucking me has an opinion in this relationship. In other words, if I'm not*

fucking; your mommy, yours sisters,
your cousins, or girlfriends then keep
their thoughts, views, opinions, ideals,
and advice out of our business. Either
that or let me start fucking them too,
and they can have their voice heard as
often as yours. You allowing Outsiders
to influence our relationships are
something we're absolutely fed up with.

• *If I can't be your Best friend then I'll*
be someone else's: A relationship
means that you and I are a team.
Although you have your girls and I
have my guys, my ultimate goal is to be
your best friend and to be mine. I want
to be your go to person and you mine.
If I can't be your go to person for; your
needs, wants, desires, heart to hearts,
shoulder to cry on, advise, physical,
financial, and inspiration then I'll go
be someone else's go to person. Evi-
dently you've got someone to take care
of you so why do I need to be here? You
know that female that always calls your
man with her problems, accomplish-
ments, and seeking his advice? If you
aren't doing the same, then guess
what? She's one up on you and a step

closer to getting your man. We take back seat to <u>No One!</u>

- *Baby Momma Drama: If he had any children prior to the two of you getting together, by chance there is a malicious, mad, vindictive Baby Momma out there somewhere. It's a great possibility that he'd never seen her horns until the two of you got serious. In any event, find a way to deal with the uneasy situation, or fold your hand. This by chance may be the toughest fight of your life but find a way to win by any means. Damn it cheat if you have to, knock her evil ass out, but prevail if I'm the one you want to be with. Remember if she were the one that I wanted to be with then I would be with her not you. You think? Anything worth having is worth fighting for.*

Chapter 8: Goals

Goals should always be one of the corner-stones when dealing with men. In the door we want to know your intentions and where we are trying to go. If there isn't some sort of set finish line that we are pushing towards, then we're only running in circles.

- *Be sure that we share the same goals: with regards to one another, i.e. open or monogamy, children or not, marriage or shacking, combined income or separate checking account, to name a few. From day one lay your cards on the table. This will enable us to decide in the door if that is the same direction that we want to go in. Don't just wing it in the beginning, and then on day your biological alarm clock goes off and you decide that you want a ring, kids, and a white picket fence. Especially when these things were never mentioned in the six months we've been seeing each other. Our defense alarm goes off. You make us feel like you've backed us in a corner. Remember that we don't do ultimatums! Ladies, let it be known from the starting gate the type of race we're running, so that there will be no misunderstanding as to where the finish line is. Men have accomplished many feats over time, but reading minds, especially those of women has yet to be done!*

- *Have some drive about yourself: just as no woman wants a dead end man. No man wants a woman who plans to go no where in life. Stop bitching and moaning about the situation that you're hating that you're in. Get off your ass, out the house, and do something with your life. We have no problem taking care of a woman who first has shown a desire to take care of her self. Make moves, show some initiative, and please stop dragging you feet. We see that as a sign of laziness. We will help you get to where you want to be if you just put forth a half ass effort.*

- *Include us in your goals: because in*

doing so you are informing me that I am who you plan to be with. By simply including us in setting and implementation of your goals only further reinforces that we are a team. That reinforcement will make us put forth that extra effort to help you achieve your goals.

- *Support us in our goals: because we have every desire to not only be successful but to also have our woman share in that success. When you don't stand behind us and support our efforts to achieve our goals you've just helped us to develop self-doubt, which is the first step towards failure. Not supporting us also tells us that you don't believe in us. Knowing that our woman is behind us is an automatic confidence booster. It will drive us to put forth that extra effort to succeed. Behind every great man stands an even greater woman; we just need to know that our Bonnie is down with Clyde.*

Chapter 9: Socializing

Never forget the fact that I had a life before you, as did you before me. I can't help the fact that there were women in my past no more than you can omit the fact that there were men in yours. That being said embrace the fact that we are together. If I wanted to be with anyone from my past I would be, lose the insecurity.

Although we are now an item, never lose your individualism, and don't try to strip me of mine.

Believe it or not, we'd love to be able to get dressed up and go out kicking it with or lady on a regular basis. We just choose to avoid it like an infectious disease at the risk of having you show your ass in public, or having to duck flying dishes when we get home. Ladies you tend to forget more often than not that when we go out together we are just that, <u>together!</u> If we are at a spot where there are other beautiful women by chance before the night is over we will have looked at a few, as would you if there are other handsome men around. To look is only a nat-

ural reaction to beauty. Stop making issues about eye gazing, when the night is over we are going home together.

If you're out and you notice that another woman has grabbed your man's attention, ask yourself these questions for the possible reasons before you decide to show your ass:

- *Q: Is the other woman dressed so scantily and showing off enough skin that anyone including you would look?*
  A: It's understandable.

- *Q: Does she look the way you used to look before you got complacent, and stopped doing the things it took to get you there?*
  A: Get it in gear and do what it takes to remain the sole apple of my eye.

- *Q: Is she just truly beautiful and worth admiring?*
  A: Then don't hate, it'll ware off in a minute or two.

- *Q: Do they have history of some sort?*
  A: Wait until you get home and <u>ask</u> me without accusing me.

In either instance if no physical contact has been made and no number exchanged, then you absolutely have nothing to trip about. Don't act as if an attractive man has never caught your gaze before. Showing out in public or at home for that matter shows insecurity, immaturity, instability, and truly makes us find every excuse in the book not to go out with you. Be forever mindful, that the more you act out the more you make us miss the ex that we can't stand!

Make room for Guy's night out. In truth unless you've just get on our nerves, we only desire it once a month. If we need it at least once a week, by chance: you've got one foot out the door and the other on a banana peel. When you oppose Guy's night out, we'll indulge in them more often just to spite you. You opposition shows a high level of insecurity. Even if the guys I hang with are dogs in your book, trust your man and trust the fact that you're doing all that you're supposed to in order to keep him from straying. Log this quote into your memory, "What another man eats doesn't make my man shit"!

Guy's night out doesn't mean chase women night. It is no different than Girls night out (we assume?), in that we have drinks and talk about the head aches or the lack there of at home. Instead of showing disdain for us wanting to go out with the Guy's try this:

- *Pick us out an outfit that you enjoy seeing us in. Reason being we are a reflection of you, so let us represent you well.*

- *Fuck us real well before we start getting dressed. Reason being is that that orgasm will occupy our mind all night. You might even find that I cut my night short just to get home to a replay.*

- *While I'm in the shower and getting dressed fix me a light bite to eat, then tell me to have fun and send me on my way.*

- *If nothing else never ever allow us to leave home mad at you. The reason is that it opens the door to bullshit, and we are prone to step knee deep into it.*

By all means, keep a Girl's night out. You need a night out with your Girls every so often so that you can go exhale. Do it to maintain some of your individuality. If for no other reason do it so that you can hear how bad other peoples relationships are, and you can come to the realization that your shit isn't as bad as you thought. Before you go:

- *Fuck us real well before you get dressed.*

- *Call us on your return trip so that we know you're making it safely*

- *If we didn't wait up, wake us upon your return, by putting it on us again.*

*I guarantee you'll never get an argument out
of us about Girl's night out. We might even financially
support you on it!*

*In today's climate of opposites attract; beware
of the potential bumps in the road down the line. If we
come from two different worlds, remember that in the
days to come. We quickly notice when you don't want
us intermingling within you social circles, because
you come up with excuses to either attend solo not to
attend functions all together. When it involves my cir-
cle you are ready to roll in an instant. Stop reaching
so far out of your social/ economical class that it
becomes a hindrance on the relationship. We truly feel
that if you're embarrassed of us then don't be with us!*

Chapter 10: Quality Time

Once again I have to stress the importance of communication with men. We are not mind readers. Communication eliminates any room for misunderstanding or misinterpretation.

Quality Time is something that Men enjoy just as much as women if not more. Our definition however may be different than yours, which are why communication is so key.

Be absolutely clear as to what one another's definition of Quality Time is. If sitting around all day Sunday, watching football, drinking beer, and eating pizza isn't your idea of Quality Time, let it be known up front. If your man is a die-hard football fan, don't schedule Quality Time on Sundays or Monday nights during football season. Six hours mall hopping isn't our idea of quality time, so don't try to pull it! Sit down and actually discuss what Quality Time means and how and when it will be implemented.

Set aside guaranteed time and don't waiver. Once you and your man have become crystal clear as *to what Quality Time is, then etch in stone when "Our Time" is and don't waiver. During "Our Time" everything else takes a back seat and nothing else gets scheduled during "Our Time" because that's just what it is, our time. You will find that over time we'll become very protective of our Quality Time, and will get hostile when it's impeded upon.*

Be creative. Don't allow Quality Time to become the same old crackers. Don't allow Quality Time to become a chore. Use your imagination and make sure that it's appealing to the both of you. Take turns planning Quality Time. Keep Quality Time spicy and different as often as possible. This way Quality Time will be something that we both will gravitate towards instead of doing it grudgingly or out of a sense of obligation.

Chapter 11: Myth Busters

With regards to Myth Busters, I will break the silence, shatter the speculation and let women know what men really think but never say. Ladies you think you know what goes on in the minds of men? Now you may have come to the realization that you didn't have a clue. By chance if you've reached this point in the book you'd really like to know, so I'm going to tell you. Here is A–Z about what men really think.

A:

* Arguments: Contrary to women's beliefs, men hate to argue. It consumes too much energy. Not to mention that words can be very hurtful, especially when said in the heat of the moment can be hurtful. Once they are said, they can't be taken back. By chance, if you continue to pick fights you'll be left to fight by yourself!

* Accusations: Stop falsely accusing us of
        things based on a hunch or a feeling. Keep
        it to yourself until you have insurmountable
        evidence. By chance, too many false accusa-
        tions will ultimately land you the proof
        you've been looking for. Yea, we'll go do the
        deed. Hell we've already gotten in trouble
        for something we didn't do so now we'll go
        do it just out of spite!

* Attraction: The things that we revealed
        attracted us to you please maintain them!
        We (just as you) have a type. Evidently you
        possessed the qualities required to meet the
        type. Although you quote unquote have your
        man; don't think that my type has changed!
        By chance, if you (out of complacency)
        begin to slack in maintaining these qualities
        we like, we'll seek to have them filled else-
        where!

* Attitude: A beautiful woman with a funky
        attitude can go from a dime to a wooden
        nickel in an instant. By chance your ugly
        attitude is the reason your fine ass is still by
        yourself!

* Abuse: Watch your mouth!
        If I don't put my hands on you, please keep
        your damn hands to yourself. By chance,
        every action results in a reaction!

B:

* **Beauty:** Above all, men love natural beauty.
  Make up should be used only to high light
  or accent your true beauty, not mask it. We
  enjoy rolling over in the morning and being
  pleased with what we see, not scared out of
  our minds because you haven't put your
  face on yet. By chance, if you continue to
  cake on make up you've got a better chance
  of landing the starring role at the circus
  than in our life.

* **Behavior:** No real man wants an alley cat. We
  are a reflection of one another. If you can't
  conduct yourself like a lady in public (no
  matter the situation), chances are you are
  clueless as to what a lady is. By chance, if
  don't know how to be a lady, you need a
  boyfriend instead of a Man. There is a difference.

C:

* **Communication:** Men are not and never will
  we be mind readers. So stop acting like we
  are and open your damn mouth and talk to
  us. Talk to us, talk to us, talk to us. I can't

*stress that enough. God gave you a mouth,
use it for something more than fussing! If
something is bothering you, tell us. If you
need something, ask us. If you feel we're
slacking, inform us. By chance, if you keep
your mouth closed, you won't get fed.*

* *Cheating: Men may <u>appear</u> to forgive but we
don't nor do we ever forget. We are highly
vindictive when cheated on. We will eventually leave but not before we leave you emotionally scarred! We will get you back. By
chance, if we cheat it's because you left your
back door open. That is you started slacking
in that which got you here! In a nutshell
you afforded us the opportunity.*

D:

* *Dependability: It's all or nothing. Either you
are behind us one hundred and ten percent
against all odds, or you can get lost! As long
as we know that we can depend on you, we'll
always be your go to guy.*

* *Dress: In three words, Sexy not Sluttish
(every man has his own individual stan-
dards)! Damn could you please leave something to our imagination? If you display all*

your goods out in public, what do we have to look forward to? Your dress will ultimately dictate the type of men you attract, and you wonder why you keep attracting Creeps! With regards to our dress, if we were dressed nice when you met us, by chance we enjoy dressing nice. So stop tripping when we dress nice to go out with the Guys.

E:

* *Eroticism: We are well aware that every woman has an erotic side. We also understand that many of you keep it suppressed for fear of either being used for it, or not being able to control it once unleashed. When in a committed relationship however, if you hold back you inform us that you don't truly trust us. If you can't trust your man enough to let your hair down and completely give all of yourself to me, then By chance you need to go find someone who can.*

* *Emotions: We have feelings too. Don't trample on ours, and by no means will we trample on yours.*

F:

* *Friends:*   *It is possible for us to have platonic female friends.*
   If we have female friends that you haven't met or aren't allowed to kick it with outside our presence, By chance, we're fucking them!
   We don't believe in you acquiring new male friends, once we're an item. It's more acceptable for you to have coffee with your male friends than drinks. If he can't come to the house, then he's more than a friend.

* *Family:*   *Keep your family out of our business!*

* *Finances:*   *We could honestly care less if a woman makes more money than we do. What we can't stand is when you attempt to use this fact to belittle us. You can honestly take your money and get the hell on*

G:

* *Greed:*   *We despise a greedy woman. We have no problem providing for your needs and most of your wants. When you start putting your wants above <u>our</u> needs, we've just fallen out of grace.*

* *Gossip:* Stop that shit. If you even entertain it you're just as trifling as the one's spreading it. We dislike our women being involved, not to mention how would you feel if you were the feature story?

* *Games:* If you never open the door, we'll never start playing them.

H:

*House: We'll play house without a ring as long as you let us. If it isn't broke don't fix it. If a ring is what you seek in the future, make it plain before we share an address.

* *Honesty:* My man Twin once told me that getting a woman to be truly honest with a man shouldn't be like pulling teeth. Stop telling me what you think I want to hear and tell me the truth. Withholding the truth is no different than telling a lie, and lies beget lies. Dishonesty will undermine a relationship. Men may not lie as good as women, but if you open the door to deceit we'll run through it head first.

I:

  * *Insecurity: A man's biggest turn off is an insecure woman. Have a backbone and stand firm on the fact that I'm with you. If you weren't the one I wanted to be with, I'd be with someone else. By chance, if you don't shake your insecurities I will be with someone else!*

  * *Independence: Maintain a certain level of independence and individuality. It shows us that you can stand on your own two feet and if necessary hold us both down if the need ever arose. If your world completely revolves around us you run the risk of smothering us.*

J:

  * *Jealousy: A touch is flattering, it let's us know that you are on point and going to protect what's yours. Too much however, evolves into insecurity, something we truly despise.*
  If you see another woman pushing up on your man, check the situation in the door. If you throw a fit every time another woman

looks at your man, you've just crossed over.
By chance, your man looks good isn't that
what attracted you to him in the first place?
Hmmm!

K:

* *Kinky:*   *We always want a freak in the bed-*
room, or any other room in the house for
that matter. If you find that you're a bit
kinkier than I am, just ease me into it, and
I'll catch on fast. No one likes a boring sex
life.

* *Kindness:*   *Discuss it with me before anything*
leaves our house or bank account. You'll
find that if we have it, we won't mind giving
to someone in need. Don't let me find out
when we need it and it's not there.

L:

* *Love:*   *Men want to fall in love, and be loved.*
We just don't want to wake up one morning
and realize that we've fallen in love with the
wrong woman. When it appears that we're
running from a commitment, we're just pro-

ceeding with caution. Just keep doing that
good stuff that you've been doing and we'll
fall like a ton of bricks. We just don't
embrace our feelings as fast as women.

* Loneliness: Just like women, what man wants
to be or feel alone?
Although it is essential that you maintain a
level of independence, make plenty of time
for me, because I require it. Or I'll go in
search of attention elsewhere.

* Lust: Men are horny by nature, if we weren't
Eve may have never been created. Satisfy my
lust as often as it arises, and we won't seek
to quench our thirst in another fountain.

M:

* Money: When we see you spend money as
fast as you get it, you show us that you have
no long-term goals, and no understanding
of what a rainy day is.
If you discover an account or stash that you
knew nothing about, By chance I don't trust
you.
Show me you can make your own and use
some to build together, instead of just
depending on mine.

* *Marriage:* *Notwithstanding financial difficulties, if I promise you a ring and more than a year passes, stop expecting it. Unless he's read this book and realizes the veil has been removed!*
  If you've been shacking for years and no ring has appeared, I'm more comfortable shacking than being married.
  Stop thinking that marriage will make it better. If our relationship is fucked up now it'll only get worse with a ring!
  If you build up the nerve to ask a man to marry you and he doesn't accept the proposal right then and there, don't hold your breath waiting for him to ask you. You will turn blue in the face and eventually pass out!

N:

* *Nagging:* *The more you nag the more you remind me that my Ex wasn't as bad as I thought. Men hate to be nagged; we'd rather have a tooth pulled. When we tell you that we will or won't do something that you ask, rest assured that it will or won't get done. There is no need to remind me every time it crosses your mind. Before you start nagging, do it your damn self if you can't wait.*

* *Nosiness:* **Stop the Super Sleuth, I Spy, Mission Impossible Shit. Quit running to answer my phone every time it rings, cracking the code to check my voice mails and text messages, calling back every unrecognizable phone number that appears on my phone bill. Keep that shit up and By chance, you just might find what you're looking for! If you don't trust me please get the hell on.**

O:

* *Orgasms:* **We enjoy them just as much as you do. We actually want to make sure that you get yours, and get them often. Communicate with us so that we understand the best way to help you achieve yours. By chance, you'll get them more often.**
  Invest in some baby wipes for easy clean up.

* *Oral Pleasure:* **Give and you shall receive! When done right, we love it as much as you do. By chance if you don't give we'll find one who will!**

* *Outgoing:* **We don't want a club rat, nor do we desire a couch potato. Be a balance between the two. Let's get up, get out, and do things together.**

P:

* *Past:*   *Stop acting naïve, we both had a past. Be truly open and honest about your past in the beginning or it will come back to bite you hard. In the end, leave the past exactly where it is, and that's in the past. Or it will corrupt your future.*

* *Purpose:*   *Why are we here? Be up front and honest about where you want to go within the relationship. If we just wing it, you'll wake up one day and realize that a lot of time has passed and the relationship hasn't gone anywhere.*

* *Peace:*   *Men love peace, and will have it at all costs. To have peace at home we feel is a right not a request. We'd rather work over-time for free than come home to drama. If you find that we are spending less and less time at home, By chance you've disrupted the peace at home and I'm getting my peace elsewhere.*

Q:

* *Quitting:*   *Finish what you start. No man wants a quitter. We'll help you if you just put forth a half ass effort.*

R:

* *Representation: You are supposed to be a reflection of me as I am of you. In our absence you are supposed to represent us to the fullest. Our relationship should be worn like a badge of honor by both of us, not like an anchor. We'll know if we're being misrepresented and this violates the trust factor.*

* *Reservations: When you hold back any part of yourself, you give us the impression that you're saving a part of you for someone else. It's all or nothing.*

* *Respect: You will get no more than you come with. Disrespect a man and be prepared to be fully compensated for your actions.*

S:

* *Sex: We want it as often as we can get it. It is not a treat for good behavior, but a pillar that will cause a relationship to crumble if rationed or removed. We want it from the one we're with but will get it elsewhere if restricted!*
  If we feel that you only fuck us out of a sense of obligation instead of genuine

desire, we'll drift.
Be creative, keep it spicy so that never gets boring to either of us.

* Secretes: They are equal to lies, and violate the trust. If there is something that you feel you have to hide from me, by chance it's wrong and violates the trust and will ultimately drive a wedge in between us. Unless the secrete is a special surprise a secrete is a no, no. A secrete is a lie in disguise.

T:

* Trust: This is the concrete that a relationship has to be built on. There are enough snakes in the world; I can't have one on my hip. You are supposed to be the one person that I can trust above any other, and if I can't then I don't need you.
Once you've earned my trust and then violate it, you become the most despised person in my life, because you were the closest to me. If the trust is ever violated, it'll never be the same, so you should really cut your loses and leave now before my vindictive nature kicks in and it gets ugly.

* Teaching: Make sure that we are well informed as to; what you like, how you like

it, and how often you require it. If we can't seem to fulfill your needs, wants, and desires in the manner most pleasing to you, <u>teach us how</u>. This way you'll never have anything to complain about.

You can believe that we will keep you well informed and be willing to teach you how to keep us satisfied.

Teaching doesn't just refer to sex, but rather all aspects of fulfillment.

U:

* **Ultimatums:** *We absolutely, wholeheartedly, will resist them at all cost. <u>We don't do ultimatums!</u> We will pay more attention to a doctor's advice for a colon cleansing than your ultimatum. An ultimatum is an order and if we wanted to take orders we'd be in the military, and even then we'd be getting paid to take then. Try asking, if that doesn't work then frankly you're out of gas.*

* **Underwear:** *One week out of each month we won't complain about you wearing your Wednesday drawers. Beyond that we enjoy seeing our women in sexy undergarments. Ladies, keep your panty and bra game tight.*

V:

* Value: Above our car, our clothes, our money, or any other thing that you may think we place a high value on, men value a good woman! When you see us place more value on any of these things than on you, By chance you aren't the good woman the both of us thought you were.

W:

* Weakness: Just, as no woman wants a spine-less man. No man wants a week woman (unless his sole intention is to take advantage of her).
Times will come where we seek to draw strength from you. If we can never lean on you, if you can never hold us up when the time arises, then guess what? We don't need you, because we can do bad by our self!

* Worth: Determine your own self worth and don't allow anyone to alter your view of it. When you do it shows weakness and uncertainty in self. How can you be worth anything to me if you don't know how much you're worth to yourself?

Be certain as to what your relationship is worth to you. You will only get out of it that which you put into it.

X:

* *X Rated: We love our X Rated material: books, movies, web sites, and strip clubs. So get over it. It's harmless until you make an issue out of it! It should be no more of an issue to you, than your toy drawer is to us!*

Y:

* *Youth: It's an exaggerated misconception that men generally prefer younger women and will eventually leave you for one. More often than not, it isn't even the case.*
We generally prefer seasoned women. In the beginning you play no games, are secure with self, and generally know how to give and receive love. In a nutshell you start off being the woman that every man wants, needs, and dreamed of. What pushes a man to a younger woman is that over time you get relaxed and even complacent. You lose sight of the fact that what got you there is

the <u>minimum</u> *effort needed to keep you there. What we now see in them is what we used to see in you.*

Next your own complacency leads to your own insecurity. As I said before, insecurity is the biggest turn off.

Then the arguing and the nagging start and that's the final straw.

All these factors combined will push us to any other woman. The reason a younger woman is chosen is because they are content with that which we are willing to give or withhold, and give no headaches in return. Once you earn the crown and become Queen, do whatever it takes to keep your crown polished. If it tarnishes, it's your own fault.

Z:

* *Zero Tolerance: Men have absolutely Zero Tolerance for a fair weather woman. Be with me right or wrong, good or bad, ups or downs, or beat it.*

—*Conclusion*—

Ladies, there is no magic spell, architectural blue print, quadratic equation, or Quantum Theory that will yield the perfect relationship with a man. But, something as simple as knowing how men think with regards to key issues will greatly enhance the probability of success.

Within these pages I've attempted to shed some light on some key issues that hold a lot of weight with men. This light will keep you from wandering around in the dark getting bumped and bruised and better help you to understand men. Through this understanding you can avoid potential pitfalls that come from a lack of knowledge.

The topics discussed herein are things men wished women knew, but for some reason never told you. In a sincere effort to create some harmony amongst the sexes I decided to tell you.

Better understanding our dos and don'ts, our wills and wont's, likes and dislikes will ultimately lead to you getting along better with us. Who wouldn't want their relationship to run a bit smoother?

This book will not solve every issue that arises within your relationships with men. It's not designed to. It's merely designed to inform you of ways to avoid potential pitfalls, headaches, and heartaches. If you take heed to that which you've read and apply it you run the risk of getting a man to truly love you better.

It is my sincere hope that something within these pages is a benefit to you on your journey towards happily ever after. If you question the validity of the things I've said within these pages, ask your man or any man for that matter. If he's truly honest with you, you'll receive confirmation that that which you thought you know about men you truly had no clue!

I truly thank you for your purchase and support. I ask that you don't loan your book out, because you wouldn't want to be without it. This book will prove to be a handy on hand reference. Tell the other Ladies that they have to get their own.

For future advice regarding the minds of Men, log on to www.AskYamo.com.

Be on the look out for my next work: " White Liver, Sexcapades", Due out Nov. 2007.

Yamo.

Author Biography:

I have always been one who women sought for advice. The reason is that if asked I gave you the <u>UNCUT</u> truth even at the risk of being brutally honest. I'd always tell you what you needed to hear instead of what you wanted to hear. With the advice I give I never claim to be an expert only honest. This is only the first of many books that I intend to share with the world. With each book you'll learn a little more about me. Until then please enjoy your reading and I thank you for your purchase

YAMO.

Printed in the United States
67207LVS00001B/361-408